M000239469

The Methods of Truth Which I Use

BY

BROWN LANDONE, F. R. E. S.

Editor-in-Chief of The Victories of Civilization, and Author of How To Turn Your Desires and Ideals Into Realities, The Success Process, The A B C of Truth, Deep Down In Your Heart, The Means Which Guarantee Leadership, et cetera.

L. N. Fowler & Co.
Ludgate Circus, London

Published by
THE ELIZABETH TOWNE CO., INC.
HOLYOKE, MASS.

Printed in U. S. A.

TO YOU

To *you*, I give these thirty-one Methods and thirty-one Divine "Prescriptions."

The *Methods* teach you how to use the *Prescriptions.*

The Prescriptions are given to help *you* attain

Abundance
Beauty
Calmness
Courage
Faith
Freedom
Friends
Growth
Guidance
Harmony in Business
Harmony in Home
Healing
Hearing
Joy
Life
Love
Mateship
Passing On
Peace Within Self
Peace With Others
Perfection
Position
Power
Protection
Rest
Sight
Strength
Understanding
Unity With God
Yourself
Youthfulness

CONTENTS

Part I—To Sustain You Hour By Hour

Part II—To Dispel Mental Fog

Part III—To Grow In Spirit And Power

CONTENTS

PART I

How To Sustain You Hour By Hour

THE METHODS OF TRUTH WHICH I USE

LESSON 1

How To Begin "Being Yourself" (For The First Day)

"YE ARE not bound" (1)* for "Back of thy parents and thy grand-parents lies the great eternal will! That too is thine inheritance." (2)

So I bring you methods of the positive God! I do so because in the past we have been trying too much to attract the good we want, instead of expressing it.

When God created the heavens and earth, He did not try "to attract" what He wanted to create; He did not even search deep within Himself to realize His creation.

Instead, God *expressed* Himself to create what he wanted to create.

So you, to create what you want, should get in line with God's method.

*The numbers in parenthesis refer to the "List of Sources" in the appendix.

Express yourself, so that what you conceive by your thought will come out into actual existence as the thing or condition you desire.

The *powers* you can use are few. They are powers of mind, love, life, and action. They are always the same for they are of God. They will never fail you for God will always continue to be what He is.

The *methods* of using these powers are many—as many as there are teachers and writers and leaders. There are so many methods that you may be confused by them. In this little book I present only the methods which I have proved to be the best—that is, those which I know bring results, each in accord with its nature after its own kind.

The *instructions* for daily use—"Won't you sup with Me," and "Divine Prescriptions"—are given at the end of the book.

These methods will aid you in securing three kinds of spiritual help: one to *sustain* you hour by hour when you are busy with the work of the day; another to help you to *understand* Truth; and still another to aid you to *grow*.

I bring you methods of the radiant soul and the positive God. Every such method must work in line with God. His activity forever radiates outward, and creates His universe by manifesting His powers. You, to keep in line with God's activity, must also radiate outward, and create what you want by manifesting your powers. You can do this only by expressing yourself.

This is a book of methods, but, dear friend o'mine, a method is only a method. It is something which helps you to use *your* powers. It can help you to find what you want within yourself. It can help you to demonstrate desires as actualities and to attain results with certainty. But, if you begin to depend on it, it becomes useless. Moreover, you hinder the operation of Truth as soon as you begin to *depend* on any method, for you—as a soulbeam of the living God—do not need to depend on any method.

God is ever-active, and His only activity is that of manifesting Himself in expression. Since you are a soulbeam of God, your only mode of spiritual realization is manifestation of yourself in *expression.*

So, in beginning to use the methods which I give in this book, begin with yourself. It is your use of your powers which creates what you want. Seek the help of methods, but depend only on the expression of the God powers within you.

> "There is no noble height thou canst not climb;
>
> All triumphs may be thine——
> If, —— thou dost not faint or halt;
> But lean upon the path of God's security." (3)

Hence begin thus:

"I shine forever in the one path provided by God for me. Since it is provided for ME, no other soul can shine in my path or interfere in any way with my expression!

"And———joy of joys—I do not need to try to do the shining for anyone else, for, since each soul shines in a path of its own provided for it by God, each is supplied by God and each is the source of all its needs.

"I shine WITH others, but not for them. They shine in harmony WITH me, and not against me. I radiate from God, and so I am the source of all I need.

I didn't know - didn't dream - I the source of all I need, took many years to learn.

By EXPRESSING the God power in me, I create what I want."

"Nothing——is greater to one than one's self is", (4) and so "Nothing shall be impossible to you." (5)

LESSON 2

How To Use "I Am That I Am"

(For The Second Day)

"RESOLVE to be thyself" (6) for "when you are you, all the world will sit at thy feet, and recognize a god." (7)

In your search for Truth, you may meet a few human peacocks! They are the *mystifiers* of Truth. They strut about, and claim that they have plumbed the depth of Truth. Then they explain that they cannot reveal it to you, because you are not sufficiently advanced to comprehend it.

There are also angels of God here on earth. They are the *mystics.* They are noble in simplicity. They know profound Truth and know that it *is* simple, and they gladly reveal it so simply that you can understand it.

The Bible was written by mystics.

"I-am-that-I-am" was written by a mystic.

Although mystifiers have tried to make "I-am-that-I-am" seem very mysterious, yet it is so profound that it is simple, and so mystical that it means exactly what it says.

"I-am-that-I-am" is very simple; it means "*I am I.*"

God knows that He *is* He, and hence He knows that He *has* power and *dares* to use it.

My consciousness of power resides in my knowledge that *I am I!*

Your power resides in knowing that "You are you!"

It is all very simple, for "Is it not written———ye are gods?"

Then dare to be one!

Dare to express your desire for activity and your body will be radiantly healthy! Dare to express your capacities and you will be flooded with abundance! Dare to express your love, and the joy of others will enfold you.

Use "I am that I am" in this way:

"I AM I; I have a right to be myself. I mount the throne which God provided for me when He gave man dominion

all the equipment & dare to use it,

over all things! I have the power of God in me, and dare to use it. "I AM I!"

"I exist as I am, that is enough!" (8) for "The Spirit of the Lord is upon me!" (9)

LESSON ·3

How To Take The Right Attitude Toward God And Yourself

(For The Third Day)

"EARTH'S crammed with Heaven and every common bush afire with God", (10) and so "The clouds that hover o'er us are only angels' wings." (11)

If you are a scientist, trying to list the hundred thousand qualities of the sunshine which streams in at your laboratory window, you will forget to enjoy it while thinking so much about it.

Yet, walking on hillsides flooded with sunshine, you will *accept* the fact that the sun does shine and you will *feel* its warmth and joy without thinking anything definite about it.

There's a lesson in this.

You have tried to "think and think and think" of God's qualities, but since

His qualities are infinite, you have not been able to think very concretely of such infinity. And so, you often fail to feel the joy of God's presence.

You get the greatest benefit of the sunshine by *letting* yourself feel its invigorating warmth instead of trying to think of its many qualities. So instead of trying to think so much of God, it is better to take the same attitude toward God that you take toward sunshine! *Accept* the Truth of God's presence just as you accept the presence of sunshine, and then you will begin to *feel* His presence. You will come closest to God by knowing that His sunshine forever surrounds you. Hold to this attitude toward God; it warms the heart, and that is more helpful than mere thoughts about God.

As to yourself, you are a soulbeam radiating out from God—from eternity to eternity. You manifest in your body but are never limited to it. The qualities of your soul are *mindbeams* of God, *lovebeams* of God, *lifebeams* of God. They give you health, happiness and riches, in proportion to your expression of them.

"I accept God's presence surrounding me, just as I accept the presence of sunshine about me. My heart knows that God is here within me and round about me. That is sufficient unto the day, sufficient unto my need!"

"There is no need to search so wide—
Open the door and stand aside—
Let God in!" (12)

LESSON 4

How To Affirm Yourself *To* What You Want.

(For The Fourth Day)

"THY THOUGHTS shall be established," (13) for "I have called thee by thy name; thou art mine." (14)

If you positively think, "I have the vitality to be healthy," you make an affirmation of health. And if you positively think, "I have capacity to create abundance", you affirm your consciousness of supply.

If, hour after hour, you continue to think and assert that you have the vitality to be healthy, you hold-a-thought of health; and if, day after day, you keep on thinking that you have the capacity to meet your needs, you hold-a-thought of supply.

An "affirmation" is a *positive assertion* of the existence of the divine means of obtaining what you want.

"Holding-a-thought" is a prolonged and *continued* affirmation.

Whether your affirmation succeeds or fails depends (1) on your recognition of what possesses the moving power; and (2) on the extent of your use of that motive power.

If my automobile is in perfect condition and supplied with oil and gas, I have a right to expect that it will run the two miles to town.

But, no matter how perfect the condition of my car or how well it is supplied with oil and gas, I have *no* right to expect that the *town* will run the two miles to my car!

In the case of the automobile and the town, it is not the town but the *car* which possesses the moving power. In your use of Truth, it is not the affirmation, but *you* who possesses the motive power.

So if you try to pull or attract things or conditions to you, you antagonize your own nature, for the only divine activity which God has given to you is His own power of moving outward—the power of radiating outward into expression.

"Every man shall receive his own reward according to his own labor," (15) and so an affirmation works successfully when you affirm *your* capacities in relation to the thing or condition you want. You are the divine moving power; consequently, instead of trying to affirm the thing or condition *to you*, affirm yourself *to it!* As you affirm that you have the power and capacity to obtain or secure the thing or condition you want, you will move yourself out toward it, and get it. It is affirmation in action which brings results.

For instance, the affirmation—"I have a divine right to enjoy God's sunshine"—always works when you, as the moving power, go out into the sunshine. But, the same affirmation fails every time you shut yourself up in a dark windowless cellar, and try to pull the sunshine in through the damp stone walls.

Actuality is always the result of action. And since you are the motive power, it is your action which gives birth to actuality. Don't try to pull the sunshine to you; go out into the sunshine of action. Then your affirmations will become actualities.

"I am radiated into infinite activity by God. My one divine activity is to express myself. As I let God's activity push me into action to obtain and attain what I affirm, I turn my affirmation into an actuality. I AM the motive power of all I want. I affirm MY activities outward to get what I want. This moment my soul goes out to take possession of that which I affirm is divinely mine."

"Whatever we think, we are;
And whatever we are, we do," (16)

LESSON 5

How To Affirm In Love

(For The Fifth Day)

"Attainment hangs but on the measure
Of what thy soul can *feel*." (17)

IN HELPING yourself, the one purpose in using affirmation is to unify some good thing with yourself and make that unity permanent. You affirm health only because you do not wish yourself and health to be separated from each other.

To bind one condition to another, the right kind of spiritual cement must be used to hold them together. Mind merely asserts; love is the spiritual cement which unifies and holds together.

If you mentally reach out for the thing or condition you want, and declare that it must come to you, it may back away and leave you! It may even leave you in a worse condition than before you attempted to grab it. I have known people to affirm abundance so assertively that they lost even that measure of abundance which they had had.

But if you reach out for what you want with a joyously expectant heart—if you *love* what you want as your own—it gladly becomes your companion. True affirmation takes place deep in your heart of love.

"I love each thing or condition which I affirm as mine. I love it so much that I af-firm myself to it—that is, I bind myself to it by love so that it is mine."

"Love is the fulfilling of the law." (18)

LESSON 6

How To Use "Denials"

(For The Sixth Day)

"Defeat may serve as well as victory
To shake the soul and let the glory
out." (19)

OFTEN it is useless to "deny" things and conditions and sometimes it leads to soul-deception and spiritual dishonesty.

If I have a wart on the end of my nose, it is spiritually dishonest for me to deny the existence of that wart. When I stand before a mirror, and positively deny that that wart exists on my nose, I know—every time I look in the mirror—that that wart *does* exist. If I continue such "denial" of a thing or condition, I build up within myself a basis of soul deception and a state of spiritual dishonesty.

Yet, there is a divine method of using "denials" which works miracles.

First, *do not deny things or conditions outside of yourself* when your conscious mind knows that they do exist. If you do so you will build up soul deception within yourself which will hinder your use of Truth.

Second, *always deny any lack within yourself;* deny that you lack the vitality to be healthy; deny that you lack the capacity to produce abundance; deny that you lack the love to win the happiness you want. In other words, always use denials in relation to *yourself.*

"I do not deny hindering conditions or things, but I do deny that I lack the power to handle them; I do deny that I lack power to remove them. There is no lack of God-power within me, and that makes all things possible with God!"

"I rave no more 'gainst time or fate,
For, lo! My own shall come to me." (20)

LESSON 7

How to Hold a Thought

(For The Seventh Day)

"With each strong thought . . .
Invisible vast forces are set thronging
Between thee and that goal." (21)

"HOLDING-A-THOUGHT" is very helpful when your mind is wobbly—that is, when your mind is uncertain as to conditions, or when circumstances make you doubt, or when you need help in sticking to an ideal.

But, as soon as your desire or ideal is determined, it is not wise to continue to hold to the thought. Thought is a *stream* of consciousness which flows forever forward into action. So if you hold to a thought of what you want for too long a time after you are certain of what you want, the "holding" may *stop* your progress, and you may be held *by* the thought.

Many teachers criticize this method, yet, I know that holding-a-thought is of great value, (1) if you use it in the right way to *steady* your mind; and (2) if you *stop* holding the thought as soon as your ideal of what you want becomes clear and certain.

If you merely repeat a thought of Truth it may become so fixed that it will kill its own creativeness and then it will fail to create what you want.

Therefore, in holding-a-thought—from hour to hour and from day to day—add some *new* idea every time you repeat it. *New* thought creates. New Thought is always creative. It will create that which you desire. Hold-a-thought so that it will continue to be creative. Let the thought *grow*, each time you use it!

"Be ye transformed by the renewing of your mind." (22)

LESSON 8

How to "Speak the Word" and "Declare" Your Freedom

(For The Eighth Day)

"THOU SHALT also decree a thing, and it shall be established unto thee." (23)

The Gospel of Saint John was written by a great mystic; and so the verse —"The words that I speak unto you, they are spirit"—contains a mystic Truth.

In this verse, the Greek word which is translated "speak" means *to send forth or to put into action.*

And the word which is translated "words" means *unseen powers.*

So in this verse, John means, "*The unseen powers which I send forth unto you, they are Spirit.*"

The "word" used in John 1:14 and that which is used in John 6:33 do NOT mean a spoken word made up of sounds, or a written word composed of letters.

In another verse, the Greek word

LOGOS is translated "word," and at the time Saint John used "logos," it meant *spiritual substance.* It was the spirit-substance which was made flesh.

So, whenever you speak the "word" for health, or abundance, or happiness, *send forth your unseen powers of spirit into action,* and "declare" that spirit-substance shall be made actuality (flesh).

"To declare" means *to make clear.* The only clear thought of freedom is freedom of action. Since you are like unto God and radiated by Him, His activity *impels* you to express freely and fully the divinity of your soul.

"I see with divine clearness, I declare that I AM a ray of God, radiated by God Himself. God IS manifesting in me. I speak the word of my freedom—send out my unseen powers into action — and thus attain the sublime freedom to which my soul has a right!"

"There is no chance, no destiny, no fate,
Can circumvent or hinder or control
The firm resolve of a determined soul." (24)

LESSON 9

How to Use Your "Divine Right" to All Good Things

(For The Ninth Day)

"Truth is within ourselves: it takes no rise From outward things." (25)

GOD is a God of justice.

It is just that you should be healthy; but is it *not* just that you should be healthy if you disobey the laws of health. It is just that you should possess abundance, but it is not just that you should have abundance, if you waste your energies or fail to use your capacities. It is just that you know happiness, but it is not just that you should be happy if you fail to express love.

God's one divine activity is radiation. Your one divine activity is expression. God has a divine right to everything which He creates by expressing Himself. You have a divine right to everything which your soul manifests in expression.

All things are yours by expression of the God power in you. That power is infinite and always supplies the capacity to get what your soul wants.

"Everything or condition to which I affirm my divine right is mine by right of my expression of myself in bringing the thing or condition into existence. In this consciousness of God's justice, all things work together WITH God, so that all things are possible to the God within me."

"And God said, Let us make man in our image—and let them have dominion." (26). And so "We should be called the sons of God." (27)

LESSON 10

How to Demand What You Want and Get It

(For The Tenth Day)

"Thought is a magnet; and the longed-for pleasure
Or boon, or aim, or object, is the steel!" (28)

TO "DEMAND" what you want *from* God is a mistake, because it assumes that God is so thoughtless that He neglects to give you what you need unless you insist on having it; or else it assumes that God is so selfish that He intends to deprive you of that which is yours unless you demand that He change His selfish intention. Certainly such assumptions are mistaken.

God made all things and consecrated all that He made for man. God is forever radiating all that which exists and all that which He creates is always present and ever ready for you to use.

Demanding what you want *from* God is wrong in method, because it is silly to "demand" from God that which He has already given you. Why stand in the middle of a room in which electric lights are blazing brilliantly, and demand that the lights be turned on? *"It shall come to pass, that before they call, I will answer."* (29)

Since God has given you divine power, and rule and dominion over all things, make your demands *of yourself!*

If you wish health, demand that your soul shall express itself more freely. If you want bodily peace, demand that you stop your mental fighting. If you want more vitality, demand that you use the energy which God has already given you. If you are rheumatically stiff, demand that you actively express yourself as much as you can now, and then such action will lead to more and freer activity.

If you wish more abundance, demand that you use *all* of your capacities instead of the few which you have been using. If you want a position, demand that your soul stop "striving to get a position," and seek *work* to be done because you love to work.

If you wish more happiness, demand that you express more love and cheer and joy and mirth—for the best of the earth will always open their arms to any child of joy!

Demand is a spiritual law. God has given it to you to use on yourself. Do so, and the powers of God within you will work miracles!

"God has given me dominion over all things. He has given me all things for my use! He said so! I demand that I use my capacities and awaken my divinity to use what God has given me to attain to what I want."

"Your heavenly Father knoweth that ye have need of all these things." (30)

PART II

How To Dispel Mental Fog

LESSON 11

How to Understand "All Is Mind."

(For The Eleventh Day)

"WHEN half-gods go, the gods arrive." (31)

An abbreviation is a shortened form of a word or phrase, with something left out. For illustration, "BL" is a shortened form of Brown Landone, with "*rown*" and "*andone*" left out.

A shortened form is easily understood if you know what is left out. But, if you do not know what is omitted, it may lead to much misunderstanding. For instance, if a stranger who did not know my name, heard me called BL, he might think that I was Mr. Bee Ell!

"All is mind" is two shortened *forms* put together. So, those, who do not know what is left out, often misunderstand it and sometimes ridicule it.

First, the word "all" is a shortened form. The words which are left out are "that which exists"—for certainly, we mean "All that which exists is mind."

Second, the little word "is" is a shortened form. The word "is" by itself is never complete. Whenever "is" is used, something else must always be added to complete the idea—such as: is good, is tall, is lovable.

In the sentence, "Man is divine," the word "is" tells us the quality of man due to his divine source. In the sentence, "All is mind," the word "is" means the quality of that which exists due to its *source* in mind.

"Wisdom is the principal thing; therefore get wisdom; and with all thy getting get understanding." (32)

Certainly, we do not mean that the chair in which you sit is mind itself. Instead, we mean that mind is the *source* of the chair—for the chair was created in mind by some idea of a chair before it was made as an actual chair.

All things made by man — whether steamship or chair, railroad or icebox —were first created in the mind of man. All things made by God— whether atom or star, cell or man — were first created in the mind of God.

To prevent confusion of thought, it is always wise to use the complete form of a Truth, instead of using its abbreviation or a shortened form. "Mind is the source of all that which exists," is the complete form of "All is mind!"

"I know that each thing has its SOURCE in mind. So, whatever I want, I conceive it first in mind. When I do this I get in line with God's method and take the first step in creating all that there is of riches, or health, or happiness. God IS spirit. All things were made BY Him (Spirit) . . . . and OF His (Spirit) all things consist."

"All things were made by Him; and without him was not anything made that was made." (33)

LESSON 12

How to Understand "Matter"

(For The Twelfth Day)

"I have said that the soul is not more than the body,
And I have said that the body is not more than the soul." (34)

AS I lie on my back on the lawn under my great catalpa tree, and look *up* at that tree, I say, "Its branches are so gigantic that they cover half the sky."

But when I mount a thousand feet in an airplane, and look *down* at that tree, I say, "It looks like a tiny shrub."

Some people, looking *outward from* the center of consciousness, say, "All is matter." Others looking inward, say, "All is spirit!" Each viewpoint is a part-view only, and each statement is a half-Truth only!

There is but one way of knowing the whole Truth about matter. It is God's way—for He made all that exists and hence He is the only absolute authority as to the nature of what He created.

God radiates but *one* substance. That one substance is all there is. It is both matter and spirit. Physical scientists know that matter is whirling spirit and spiritual scientists know that matter is spirit in manifestation. Matter *is* spirit, and spirit *is* matter.

Our differing ideas of matter and spirit are due to *our* attitudes or positions. But, God's substance is God's substance—no matter what *you* call it, or what your opinion or limited viewpoint may be.

Understand matter as God knows it. God conceives a thought of salt. God expresses His thought, and salt exists! Salt is conceived of God as a thought; it is expressed of God as substance, and hence, it *must* be God-thought in manifestation.

"And God saw everything that He had made, and, behold, it was very good." (35)

All matter is divine, God gave you rule and dominion over it, not to condemn all things, but to bless them, and use them — because He blessed them, and gave them to you for your use. This ideal is necessary for abundance. You can create poverty for yourself by condemning matter and material things— for what you condemn turns away from you. You create riches by blessing all things as God blessed them.

"I no longer condemn matter or material things. Instead, I bless them, just as God blessed everything He created, and declared everything to be "very good." I bless all things, and they love me, and become mine!"

"Be ye glad and rejoice forever in that which I create." (36)

I bless and attract

and thus "create,

LESSON 13

How to Understand the "Subconscious"

(For The Thirteenth Day)

"Can He be held in our narrow rim?
Do the work that is work for Him—
Let God Out!" (37)

"SUB" MEANS *under*, and consequently the word "subconscious" is a misleading term. The subconscious is not under anything. It is not under the conscious mind — not even under the conscious mind's direction.

Yet, we use the word subconscious for the same reason that we use other words which have lost their original meaning. "Manufactured" means made by *hand*, yet we use it to mean things made by machinery, because that meaning is understood, and because the one purpose of all language is to make oneself understood.

So also, since there are no better terms, we still use the terms "subconscious mind" and "conscious mind," although there is but *one* mind. When I use "conscious mind," I mean the conscious *activity* of the one mind. When I use "subconscious mind," I mean the subconscious *activity* of that same mind.

You are a stream of mind flowing out from God. At this moment, you are conscious of some state of activity of your mind. Tomorrow you will be conscious of some other state of activity. The conscious activity of your mind embraces all mind activities which you recognize now, or now remember as of the past, or now vision as of the future.

And what is subconscious activity? Remember that you are a *stream* of mind flowing out from God—from forever in the past to forever in the future. Consequently the subconscious is not a hidden lake, nor a reservoir of power! It is the great *ever-lasting flow of life* from God, supplying and sustaining you, and urging you on to greater expression of yourself.

You do not tap its power by going into trances, because God's one activity is radiation and your one divine activity is expression. Hence, the more you keep in line with God by expressing yourself, the more you will open up the channel of subconscious activity, for all power—conscious or subconscious—comes into manifestation by expression!

The subconscious activity of my soul is the sum total of all the powers and knowledge acquired in my infinite *flow* from the eternity of my past with God up to my present moment of consciousness with Him. Since all power is of *one* mind, my subconsciousness cannot fight my consciousness.

"My subconscious mind is a stream, flowing to me with all the power of God. It gives ME power infinitely greater than that of my conscious mind. With its help coming from God, all things are possible."

"The Lord thy God in the midst of thee is mighty." (38)

LESSON 14

How to Understand and be Free of "Mortal Mind"

(For The Fourteenth Day)

"Here on the common human way
Is all the stuff the gods would take
To build a Heaven." (39)

WHEN you understand just *what* "Mortal mind" actually means, you can be free of every fear of its influence.

"Mortal mind" is a strange phrase. "Mortal" means that which ends in *death*, and "mind" is spirit which *lives* forever.

So if mortal mind means anything, it must mean "something which lives *forever* and at the same time *ends* in death!" It is a double contradiction: mortal contradicts mind, and mind contradicts mortal. One might as well try to explain "a sun which shines forever and never shines."

Even those who teach it, *subconsciously* know that it has no meaning. That is why they resort to the "sign" of *m* contrasted with *M*, to try to put some meaning into it. If it had a real meaning even to their minds, they would not find it necessary to use such a sign.

And yet, they teach you that there is a malicious mortal mind always ready to influence you; that it is an illusion which does not exist; that your sins are errors due to its vicious ideas; and that you should beware of it and protect yourself from its malicious magnetism.

If you really fear it, repeat what follows; it will cure every fear of mortal mind. I guarantee it:

"There is a vicious cow in my bedroom always ready to harm me; it is an illusion of a cow which does not exist; I must beware of it and protect myself from the maliciousness of that cow which does not exist!"

"I fear no mortal mind—for I fear no cow that does not exist! There is but one God, and I AM a soulbeam of His sunshine. He radiates me forever. There is naught for me to fear!"

"Thou hast given him power over all flesh." (40)

"That whicb was Good
Doth pass to Better—Best." (41)

LESSON 15

How to Understand Sin and Sickness

(For The Fifteenth Day)

"WHATEVER happens to anybody it may be turned to beautiful results." (42)

Sin is that which for a time misses the mark of what you desire to be or attain. Certainly I do not commend it; but neither do I condemn it. It is a *lack*, and the more conscious your soul becomes of its lacks, the more your soul will want to make your manifestation of its divine nature complete in expression.

I do not condemn sin, because I know that it is a *voice* urging me to express more fully the spirit of truth in me.

Sickness is the result of repressing your soul powers.

I do not deny it, because each illness is a *voice* telling me of some lack of activity, or some lack of wisdom in living, or some lack of love in expression.

Sin and sickness are not punishments. They are *lacks*. They are due to your failure to express in fullness the divinity of the God within you.

When you do express freely and fully, sin and sickness cease for you.

"There is a high place in the upper air,
So high that all the jarring sounds of Earth
Melt to one murmur and one music there."

(43)

LESSON 16

How to Understand "There Is No Evil"

(For The Sixteenth Day)

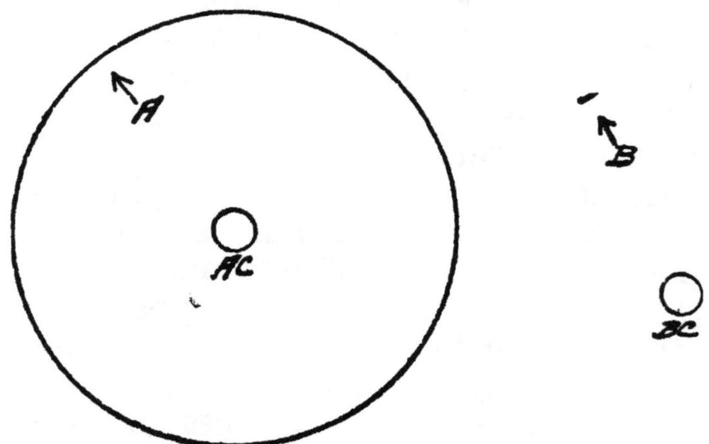

"A" represents The Perfect Circumference of The Perfect Circle of the Life of each Soul, as it is seen by God, and as it is! AC is its center.

"B" is a tiny part of the *same* Perfectly curved Circumference. It "seems" to be straight, because *you* fail to see the rest of the circumference, and see only the little part marked "B." BC is the center of the Circle, which would appear if you should continue the little line B.

BLESSED are the pure in heart, for they shall see God (Good). (44)

Whenever you perceive only a part of a condition or an activity, you may mistake its purpose, and call it "evil."

Let me make this Truth clear. Place a saucer on a piece of paper. Draw a light pencil line around it—the outline of a circle much larger than the Circle "A" on this page. When you see that curved line in its completeness, you know that every part of that line *is* curved, and that every little section of it is part of the *perfect* boundary of the circle.

Now erase all of the circumference, except one little part a quarter of an inch long. That part is a section of a perfectly *curved* circumference. Yet it looks straight like "B", because the rest of the line is erased so that you do not see the perfect whole.

That is the way to misunderstand evil. *"On earth the broken arc; in heaven, the perfect round."* . . (45)

Whenever you feel inclined to condemn another, think of the little part of the line you drew. It doesn't look as though it were perfectly curved, yet it *is* a perfect part of a perfect circumference.

Whenever you feel inclined to think of evil in yourself, realize that today you are seeing only a tiny part of yourself, of which the complete whole *is* perfect.

"All Nature is but art unknown to thee . . .
All discord, harmony not understood;
All partial evil, universal good." (46)
"Judge not, that ye be not judged." (47)

LESSON 17

How to Understand "The Silence."

(For The Seventeenth Day)

"There is an inmost centre in us all,
Where Truth abides in fullness." (48)

MOST people mistake noise for action. That's why they misunderstand the "Silence."

A Rolls Royce in high speed at ninety miles an hour runs very quietly, but a flivver chugging along at eight miles an hour is so noisy it rasps the nerves.

The slower the activity, the more noise.

The faster the activity, the quieter it is.

Sound waves produce *all the noise* in the world. They travel only 1130 feet per second! That's the reason they make noise.

Light waves are silent. They travel 186,000 *miles* per second. That's the reason they are silent.

Infinitely rapid speed - silent.

Infinite activity is *silent*, and silence is infinitely *active.*

There is absolute Silence only in the infinite activity of God. Infinite Silence is not the deadness of a non-active calm. It is the peace of the greatest activity.

Since Silence *is* infinitely active, you cannot find its peace, by trying to "stop your thought" to become non-active. Trying to be non-active sets up a conflict within you — a conflict between your efforts to be non-active, and God's great activity within you. It is this conflict which makes it difficult for some people to realize the Silence.

"To be alone with silence is to be alone with God." (49)

Since Silence is the infinite activity of God, don't try to *go* into the Silence, but *let* the Silence come into you to manifest through you. Sit quietly if you wish—or stand or work or play—and let the Silence flow!

"Silence is the INFINITE ACTIVITY OF GOD IN ME; it is so active it is absolutely silent. It flows silently into me, without any sound, without any noise, flowing in infinite energy

The Silent Period. The Silence.

1. Don't try to "Go into the Silence".

through me, so that the noisy bother of the daily life is replaced by the infinite peace of the activity of God."

"He that dwelleth in the secret place of the Most High shall abide under the shadow of the Almighty." (50)

LESSON 18

How to Understand "The Unchanging God"

(For The Eighteenth Day)

"God is the Whole—love all and you love God;
Soul and body, sky and sea and sod." (51)

"UNCHANGING" can be applied to that which *stands still forever.*

And "unchanging" can also be applied to that which *continues in action forever.*

A ray of light travels 186,000 miles a second—so fast that you cannot imagine it. If an airplane could fly as fast as a ray of light travels, it would be able to fly seven times around the earth during the time it takes you to count "one."

The speed of a ray of light is unchangeable; the speed is always the same. Although it moves through space at a stupendous speed, it is forever unchangeable!

So, when we use the phrase, the "unchanging God," it does not mean that God forever stands still—for, in Truth, God is infinitely active and never stops His activity.

God is as unchangeable as the ages in that He never stops His ever-changing activity. He never changes to a stand-still God. It is in this that He is unchangeable!

"The way of the Lord is strength." (52)

LESSON 19

How to Understand "There Is no Death"

(For The Nineteenth Day)

"The whole world changes and I too evolve In God's own way." (53)

WHEN YOU walk from one room to another, you leave one room behind and enter another room. But you do not cease to exist merely because you pass from one room to another. You do not leave your life in the room from which you have come; it is merely the *room* you leave behind.

Death is only a doorway. You merely step through it from one room of life to another!

Or it is a gate, through which you pass from one garden of life to a garden of greater life and joy.

Passing-on is stepping-through!

Of course, passing-on is change; it is a change to greater growth and greater joy—for the law of God always compels progress.

In each apple tree in springtime, the sap is actually changed into buds; It's a miracle! The sap does not "lose" its life. Instead, its life progresses in manifestation from sap to flower, and you do not weep when sap changes to apple blossoms!

Each passing on is a step forward into a greater life, greater joy, greater expression—for all life is eternal!

Death is the *progress* of life, forever toward greater expression.

"God is life, and I am a life-beam of God radiating His life. It radiates forever; it never recedes; IT ALWAYS PROGRESSES. I have no fear of pro-

gression; I am joyously certain of greater joy and life for myself and my loved ones. All life IS eternal progression!"

"I will turn their mourning into joy —and make them rejoice from their sorrow." (54)

PART III

To Grow In Spirit And Power

LESSON 20

How to Use Visualization to Get What You Want

(For The Twentieth Day)

"WHAT I have seen—is sufficient." (55) "Brighten some bit of darkness by shining just where you are." (56)

If you had been one of my students forty years ago, you might have heard me say: "If you continually impress a perfect ideal of what you want on your subconscious mind, it will become an actuality." I used to teach each student to "fix" a *picture* of what he wanted in his mind. I used to teach that "visualization" fixes the perfect idea of what you want in your subconscious mind, just as light fixes a picture on a camera plate. I used to compare pictures in the mind with light pictures on a camera plate, because it was a "nice" illustration.

In later years I have learned that there are several "blurs" of mistaken thought in that illustration.

First, your mind is *not* like a 2″ x 3″ camera plate.

Second, a camera plate of itself stands still, because it has no power of movement within itself. In contrast, your mind is infinitely active.

Third, merely taking a picture on a camera plate is not of much value unless you develop it; and so also, impressing a perfect idea of the mind is not of great value unless you develop it by action.

And fourth, since your mind is a stream of power moving out from God with incredible and stupendous activity, nothing can be "fixed" in it or on it.

Yet visualization itself works in accord with God and produces after its own kind. Since it *is* visualization it reproduces after its own kind. Since it *is* visualization it reproduces a true vision of what you desire. This is very helpful in keeping you *on* the road of consecrated effort.

Use each power of your mind in the way God commanded you to use all things—each to produce after its own kind. Since visualization is the act of visioning, it creates a vision. Use it to create after its own kind—to form the ideal vision of what you want to do. Then *follow* the vision. But do not expect visualization to produce actualities. Use visualization to visualize what you want.

Visualize to form your ideal; then act to produce its actuality. Visualize what you want so vividly, that you *will do* whatever is necessary to get what you want. If it is a thing, mentally picture it in its colors; picture its definite form, and give it its actual size—just as you want it to be.

Then visualize yourself in action, for action is evidence of your *use* of your powers. Action results in actuality, and since you want an actual result, visualize yourself in movement—in action, getting it; in action, using it.

If you want a beautiful garden, not only picture the garden as you wish it to be, but visualize yourself in action, making the garden. See yourself physically cultivating the soil and putting the seeds into the ground. Then visualize plant life in action. See sprouts coming up. See the plants growing day by day. Visualize also your love of caring for the garden; visualize your love of watching things grow, and visualize growth as one phase of God's expression here and now!

"Though a man say he hath faith and have not works, can faith save him?" (57)

Use visualization for what it is intended to be used, but do not expect abnormal results—for Truth is normal, not abnormal. Use paints to *paint* a picture of delicious fruits, but do not expect to *eat* the picture. Use visualization to produce the true *vision* which will lead you to what you want, but do not expect to subsist on the vision.

"I visualize to create the star which will inspire and guide me, so that I shall be spurred on to reach my pot of real gold.

"My mind is a stream of power. Power would cease to be power if it were not able to DO things. I visualize what I want to impel the God-in-me to DO whatever is necessary to produce the actuality I desire. My true visualization will always lead me into the ac-

tivity which will MAKE my ideal come true!"

"Be of good courage, and He shall strengthen your heart." (58)

LESSON 21

How To Concentrate By Consecrated Thought

(For The Twenty-first Day)

"SPACE is nothing to spirit; the deed is outdone by the doing." (59)

Do not be discouraged if your thoughts become more and more scattered when you try to concentrate.

Nothing is the matter with you. It is the method which is wrong.

There is a difference between concentration of thought and consecration of thought. Carefully note the words I used. They are not the same. One is con-*centra*-tion; the other is con-*secra*-tion.

Concentration is the act of trying to focus your mental energies or ideas at a CENTER, and to keep them centered on one thought.

Consecration is the act of sacredly unifying your thoughts in an effort to accomplish a desired result or to attain a sublime ideal.

Our aim in practicing concentration has been right, but our use of the word "concentrate" has sometimes misled us, so that we have tried to hold our thoughts *to* a center. Such con-centration brings your mind to a standstill, with each thought butting its head against the others! It gets you into all sorts of trouble. If it is continued for a short time, it leads to confusion of thought, and makes you discouraged because you think you cannot learn to concentrate. If continued for a considerable time, it leads to hallucination.

"Why did the flower fade? I pressed it to my heart with anxious love, that is why the flower faded." (60)

Con-centering thought is contrary to God's law of activity for God never turns His power inward toward a center. He always radiates His power outward. So when you try to con-center your thoughts, you work directly opposite to God's mode of thought. When you try to "hold" your thoughts still at a center, God scatters them so that you will not harm yourself by such a mistaken method.

So, praise the Lord that you have *not* been able to concentrate by con-centering! Sing a Hallelujah! Sing it, because you've never learned to concentrate in that way.

What you need is consecrated effort in expressing yourself. Expression is movement outward. Consecration is action which is "alert in one direction." So instead of trying to concenter your thoughts, consecrate yourself to express yourself to the limit in doing what you most wish to do.

First, visualize the ideal *goal* which you want to reach. This determines the direction of your effort.

Second, stop trying to "hold" this ideal *in* your mind. But instead, picture it ahead of you. This impels you to go forward.

Third, picture *a direct track from you to the goal you want to reach.* This makes your mind work in one direction only.

Fourth, realize that you are an *irresistible power* moving out from God, moving along the track you visualize, toward what you want to reach. This puts you in line with God's activity.

Fifth, vision God's power *pushing* you directly toward what you want. This prevents you from switching to a side track, and impels you *to* the goal.

"Fear thou not; for I am with thee: be not dismayed for I am thy God." (61)

LESSON 22

How To Express Your Desires Freely, Without Limitation

(For The Twenty-Second Day)

"FROM this hour I ordain myself loosed of limits———my own master total and absolute." (62)

Expressing yourself freely and completely without limitation, is doing what you *most* want to do!

In this, there is freedom and the joy of being yourself.

But, in such expression of yourself, there is *no* running wild, for that limits you to expression of a mere whim and leads not to freedom but to greater bondage.

Once a young man wrote me, "How can I believe that free and complete expression of desire is right? Just now

I want money. But if I should give free and complete expression to that desire, I would rob a bank, wouldn't I?"

And I answered, "*NO!*"

Expressing desire without any limitation must give you freedom, otherwise it is not "free" expression. Robbing a bank would not give you freedom. You would be continually *bound* by fear of being found out, *hunted* by officers of the law, and *haunted* by your own consciousness.

Moreover, robbing a bank is *not* a complete expression of any soul's desire for money. Robbing a bank is *not* self expression "without limitation", for it limits not only the present but the future also.

So again I assert that free and complete expression is divine, for it prevents all limited attempts to carry whimsical desires into action. Be certain of this: No wild *whim* can give *full* expression to a soul.

"Free and full expression results in happiness. Happiness is what I most want."

"Everyone that is perfect shall be as his master." (63)

THE METHODS OF TRUTH

LESSON 23

How To "Leave It With God"

(For The Twenty-Third Day)

"DO THY duty; that is best; leave unto thy Lord the rest!" (64)

"Leaving it with God" puts the solution of your problem in mighty hands, so that you feel that you need not worry or be anxious. It makes you divinely certain of the result. It brings peace, confidence, power.

But you will be disappointed if you assume that you have a right *to dump* your problem on God!

It is right to "leave it all *with* God," but wrong to try to "*leave* it all to Him." The first attitude leads you to work with Him; the second leads you to shirk your part.

There is a difference!

If you think you can relieve your real self from the necessity of doing any thing to attain to what you want, your attitude is radically wrong, because such an attitude assumes that God's activity is *separate* from your soul's activity.

If your activity were separate from

God's activity, you would be forever damned. Such an attitude of "*leaving* it with God" makes you feel separate from God, and builds up a false faith of trusting in something apart from yourself to do something for you.

Moreover, such an attitude prevents you from recognizing your unity with God. It *limits* your consciousness of yourself to your conscious mind only. That is why your conscious mind says that you can do nothing more. It also leads you to disown the immensity and divinity of all those capacities of your soul of which you are not conscious at the moment.

"*Leaving* it to God" tries to dump something from yourself to something which is separate from yourself. Separated from God, there is failure.

But, when you "leave it all *with* God", all things are possible—for you recognize that God is with you, and that you are *with* God.

"Leaving it WITH God" is the Christ attitude. It recognizes that God is the divinity in your soul, so that you abandon all worry and anxiety of conscious effort, and leave your problem to the

stupendous divinity of God within you. Thus, your divinity WORKS with God, bringing perfect peace, wondrous calm, and stupendous power—so that all things ARE possible!

"As many as are led by the Spirit of God, they are the sons of God." (65)

LESSON 24

How To Use Realization

"The worlds in which we live are two:
The world **I am** and the world **I do.**" (66)

I USED to try to make "realization" clear to my students, by stating that "it is the mental act of making an ideal real". But after some years of such teaching, I realized that my definition did not clearly explain what *real* itself means. So I tried to find out how other teachers explained it.

Some stated that to "realize" a Truth is to know it as a divine certainty. Others taught that whatever you "realize" as a thought will of itself come to you as an actuality which you can use.

I now doubt such teaching, for although I *realize* with divine certainty that there *is* a milky-way in the sky, yet, my realization does not make that milky-way *come* to me as an actuality which I can use.

There is, however, a third meaning which gives us something practical with which to work. I found it when searching for its meaning in the writings of the ancients. The word "real" comes from an old Sanskrit word which means "from-thought-to-thing."

So, true realization is the process which leads "from-a-thought-to-a-thing!" Realization is a *process.* It begins with a thought and ends with a thing. Realization first *thinks* of what you desire and then *acts* to produce the actual thing of which you have thought. Unless you carry the process into action, you fail to practice true realization—for realization is a dual process. If you stop with the thought-half of it, and fail to use the action-half of it, you may fail to get what you are trying to realize.

In its true and complete sense, "to realize" is the same as *to actualize.* So, I ask you to study the lesson on "How To Actualize What You Want"—for realization is changing your thought into a thing by the means of thought followed by the action. Unless you make the *change*—unless you change from the thought to the action which fulfills the thought—you do not use complete realization.

In thought, I started the realization of this book which you are reading, more than two years ago. I conceived it at that time and planned each lesson. But the thought never became a thing (an actual book) so long as I felt that I did not have time to turn my thought into action. My thought is now realized because I have dictated the copy for the book and the publisher has printed it.

"Today I stop trying to get results by using half-truths! I consecrate myself to carrying my thought INTO action, just as God does. I make my realization real by action. I desire, I think, I DO—and all is mine!"

"Behold, the Kingdom of God is within you." (67)

LESSON 25

How To Idealize What You Want

(For The Twenty-Fifth Day)

"I AM the master of my fate; I am the captain of my soul." (68)

In using "idealization", you use *all* the methods given in this book—each and all of them—for the reason that idealization includes all of them.

It results in actualization—for in addition to the use of mind, and love, and life, idealization includes action!

Begin with your *desire*. Make it a divine fire, knowing that you are the source of all you want. Realize that you can create your own world by your expression of yourself, for you are divine in nature, radiating directly from God.

Then, in *thought*, conceive what you want. Make a perfect picture of it in mind. This includes visualization, affirmation, holding-the-thought, declaring what you desire, and speaking the word.

Then, *love* what you have conceived. Love your ideal as a mother loves her child, so that you will take care for it deep within your spiritual consciousness. Treasure it in your heart. Meditate on it, leave it with God; and praise the Lord for what shall come to pass!

Next, multiply and increase your activities—devising new ways by which *you* can put yourself into action to turn your desire into actuality. Unify your plan by true consecration, and become a Niagara of power in action, to bring your ideal into existence.

Lastly, *act*, and keep yourself in action until you have attained the thing or condition you want.

Idealization is the complete process of using Truth. But, since the last phase of idealization—actualization—has been neglected so much in the past, I devote the next lesson to this step—the one and only process which turns a desire into actual reality.

First, *desire* what you want with all your heart.

Second, *in thought*, conceive what you want.

Third, *love* it, as a mother loves her child.

Fourth, *multiply* all the means and methods you can use to bring it about.

And fifth, *act* and keep yourself in action to turn your thought into the actual thing or condition you desire.

These five processes form the method of idealization. When you use it, you work with God, and all things are possible.

"He made him lord of his house, and ruler of all his substance." (69)

LESSON 26

How To Actualize What You Want

(For The Twenty-Sixth Day)

"GOD IS a thing you have to do." (70)

A wish is a *mental* whim, and hence it is often impossible of fulfillment. I may wish that my old dressing gown were new again, but such a wish will never come true.

A desire comes from the *heart.* It is a longing to fulfill a want. I desire a new dressing gown to take the place of the old one. Desires are possible of attainment.

A want is recognition of a *spiritual need.* Its fulfillment is always possible.

Seek to fulfill what your spirit most *wants*. Then all other things shall be added unto you, for—when you recognize the divinity of your soul—you will desire only that which you *most* want, and thus establish the perfect unity of desire and need and supply.

As soon as the desire is certain, as soon as the ideal is perfectly conceived, as soon as it is divinely loved, as soon as you have multiplied your plan of attaining it—get into action, for there is no way of producing an actual condition or thing, except by action. Action is God's means of making ideals come true.

Affirm enough to strengthen yourself, but do not spend so much time in affirmation—or realization, or visualization—that you have little time left for action. Action produces actuality, and actuality is God in manifestation.

"God produces actuality by action; I am a soulbeam-of-action, I stream out from God in continuous activity, and hence nothing can stop my activity! Any activity—based on desire, thought, and love—will produce actuality!"

"Seize this very minute;

What you can do, or dream you can, begin it;
Boldness has genius, power, and magic in it!
Begin, and then the work will be completed." (71)
"Who will render to every man according to his deeds." (72)

LESSON 27

How To Meditate

(For The Twenty-Seventh Day)

"MY PRESENCE shall go with thee". (73)

Years ago I often advised students to meditate on a Truth. I presume I gave such advice to thousands, and I always thought that my advice was definite, until one day a young man asked "How do you meditate?" And then, when I started to answer, I realized how indefinite the process was even to my own mind. When he pinned me down, about all I could say was: "I just sit still and calmly think about the truth on which I wish to meditate."

Then he asked, "But, *how do you think* to make it meditation?"

And, frankly, I could not answer him. Although I had meditated on Truth for years and had found it very helpful, I could not say anything more definite than, "Why I just meditate."

So, then and there I consecrated myself to find out *what* meditation really is.

I studied the *derivation* of the word "meditation" and found that the highest authorities do not agree. Some think that it comes from a root which means artistic designs, while others think that it is derived from a root which means cows!

I studied *definitions*: One is "close-thought" but that is not very clear for no dictionary tells us what kind of thought is close! Another definition is "revolving in the mind" but "revolving" itself is defined as turning round like a wheel!

I read many *books* on the subject, but although such books confirmed my own experience of the great spiritual value of meditation, not one of them gave a definite statement of *what* meditation is.

I wrote to *other teachers* of Truth,

asking them what they did when they meditated, and the best answers I received were, "Why———just quietly think and meditate." These were just as unsatisfactory as the answer I had given to the young man who had asked me the question.

It was astounding! All of us meditated. All of us derived great spiritual benefit from it; yet none of could define the process, except to state that "meditation is the act of meditating," which is no clearer than saying that "condexpretestion is the act of condexpretessing."

So, let us do a little clear thinking for ourselves.

First, meditation is some kind of thinking.

Second, it is *not* argumentative thought, or reasoning, or willing, or imaging, or remembering or forming judgments.

Third, although it is not repetition of thought, yet, it is a kind of running-along-process of thinking; it is thinking of a Truth again and again; and yet it is more than mere repetition.

Fourth, the thought which you obtain as a result of meditation is *not* in the *same form* as the thought with which you begin to meditate!

When I had gone through these processes of thinking, a light dawned. Then I began to realize just what I do when I meditate, and what others do when they meditate.

In meditation I begin with a certain thought of Truth, but before I have finished, I have changed the form of that Truth so that it fits my case and helps me to meet my problem. I change it so that it is really a part of my soul's self.

The process is much like this: you go to a store, buy a few yards of beautiful cloth, go home and make the cloth into a beautiful dress which fits you, and—in fact, becomes a part of yourself in your expression to others.

There's a difference between yards of cloth and the dress which fits you. The cloth represents the materials of Truth on which you meditate; the dress represents the results of the meditation.

Meditation is that method of thought which mystically *changes* a statement of Truth so that it fits your problem, and so that it becomes a part of your consciousness—an actual part of your own spiritual thought!

"I consecrate myself to the use of the truth of these lessons. Each day I meditate on one of the truths of this book, modeling it to FIT my own problem, to help me understand what I should do to attain what I wish. Since I am a creator, I re-make each Truth into a new form to fit my need—to help me in my expression."

"He shall have dominion also from sea to sea, and from the river unto the ends of the earth." (74)

LESSON 28

How To "Praise God"

(For The Twenty-Eighth Day)

"It isn't raining rain to me,
It's raining daffodils." (75)

IF THE praise you give to God is a sort of *receipt*—given for things for which you have asked and which He has delivered to you—your receipt may stand in a court of the law, but it will not be accepted by God as praise from your heart, and it will not lead to happiness and health and abundance.

Then also if the praise you offer to God is given merely as a promise of appreciation, given in anticipation of what you ask Him to give you, it may be little more than a spiritual bribe!

Oh, praise God as the Bible tells you to praise Him! The Hebrew word translated praise means, "being exceedingly joyous". Be joyous for things as they are.

I seldom guarantee any method, but I *do* guarantee results if for one half minute, every waking hour for a month, you praise God with mirthful joy, as follows:

"I praise you, God, that I have not one hundred feet, and hence do not have to lace and unlace fifty pairs of shoes every night and morning!

"And, when I unwisely eat too much pie, I praise you, dear Lord, because you have given me only one stomach, instead of seven!

"And, I praise you because canary birds sing, instead of cough!

"And my heart is mirthful every minute—I mean it, dear Lord, *every* minute—because you made the sun golden yellow, instead of a liverish brown.

"Each moment my heart sings with joy, because things *are* as they *are!*"

If you use such praise, for half a minute every waking hour for a month, I guarantee that your whole attitude toward life will be changed! I guarantee it! For the little things you think are wrong are unimportant compared to the millions of things that are right as they are!

Praising the Lord is "being exceedingly joyous". David, the beloved of God, was a joyous singer, praising God in a thousand songs. David was so joyous that he even *danced* with joy before the Sacred Ark when it was carried through the streets to be placed in the Holy of Holies!

"I change my ideas to God's ideal: Mirthful joy is holy!"

"I will sing praises unto the Lord." (76)

LESSON 29

How To "Be Spiritual".

(For The Twenty-Ninth Day)

"Let thine own soul's light shine on the path of hope,
And dissipate the darkness." (77)

AFTER many years I have found that one thing is more worthwhile than all others—to give up fretting about little things, and to fulfill Christ's purpose—to be joyously happy.

Nineteen hundred years have passed since Christ told us that He came that His joy might be fulfilled in us. We have longed to be spiritual and have tried faithfully to become spiritual. Yet we have failed to be "filled" with joy—for the world is not yet happily joyous!

Therefore, something is wrong with our method, so let us get understanding.

Truth is *recognition* of man's divinity.

Spirituality is its *expression!*

Man is made in the image of God, so the more he represses his soul power, the *less* spiritual he becomes.

Yet, for ages people have tried to become spiritual by repression. Even today—some refuse to eat meat; others will not eat salt with food; others will not use buttons on their clothes; others will not drink coffee, or play cards, or dance.

Every such repression is based on a *materialistic* ideal, and not on a spiritual ideal. Each such attitude puts the soul's divinity on a *lower level* than that of meat, salt, buttons, or coffee. When a soul born of God "thinks" that a cup of coffee has more power than his soul, it has sunk to the depths of materialism.

God's only manifestation is in His expression. Instead of vainly trying to become spiritual by *not* thinking this or that, or *not* doing this or that, or *not* using this or that, change to God's way! Express more of mind, love, and life!

"Today I am LIKE God; God expresses Himself; spirituality is God in expression; I AM like God and hence I dare to be God-like. Expression is the only spiritual activity of man.

"Stand fast in the faith, quit you like men, be strong." (78)

LESSON 30

How To Be Conscious of "Unfaltering Faith."

(For The Thirtieth Day)

"Nor time nor space, nor deep nor high,
Can keep my own away from me." (79)

IT IS not strange that the only trouble with your faith is that you foolishly deny that you have what you have!

You always *have* faith. Every time you take a mouthful of food, you prove that you possess great faith! Every time you buy a ticket at a railway station, you have faith that the conductor will accept that ticket for fare. Every time you ask to have goods delivered from a store, you prove your faith.

Every activity of every moment of your life proves that you have faith! Why then, do you say that you lack faith? It is silly to deny that you have that which you hourly prove that you have.

You do not need to seek faith; but you may need to awaken your conscious mind so that it will *know* that you have faith; and since you have it, you can make yourself conscious of it.

So, whenever you foolishly feel that you lack faith, begin to record on a sheet of paper, the thousand things you do, hour by hour, moment by moment, each of which proves that you already have unfaltering faith, and depend on it. Keep such a list for one day and you will become conscious of your faith!

"God is forever radiating outwards; and I am forever manifesting Him. I know that God is eternal and will last forever. So, I have absolute faith that He will shine forever, and so shall I!"

"Whatsoever ye shall ask in prayer, believing, ye shall receive," (80) for "He dwelleth with you, and shall be in you." (81)

LESSON 31

How To Become A Niagara Of Power.

(For The Thirty-First Day)

"WHO BETTER than I should know——the wonderful hidden sources of your strength beneath?" **(82)**

Streams of stupendous power flow outward forever from God. They never cease. They are unlimited in number —there are trillions and quadrillions of them. Each stream is a soul flowing from God. Each stream is a gigantic Niagara of Spirit. You are such a stream of power direct from God Himself. You have the power of a gigantic spiritual Niagara.

But you do not believe it; you merely *assert* it at times— and that is what causes your seeming lacks.

You doubt because even when you faithfully assert that all power is yours, it doesn't seem reasonable. Yet, if you did understand it, you could and would believe it. And if you could and would believe it deep in your heart, you would always be conscious of power to move mountains. So, let me help your unbelief.

You doubt because you limit your vision of Truth by thinking of separation of power, instead of expanding your vision of unity of action. Whenever you compare God's power to your power, it is necessary for your mind to separate God's power from your power in order to make any such comparison.

Even when thinking of yourself as a Niagaric stream of power, you are likely to think "but I'm only a drop in the stream."

Well, what of it! As a single drop by yourself alone, you can do nothing. Christ has said so, and it is so sensible that no one teaches that you have all power if separated from God.

But with unity of action with God, all power is yours.

Even as one drop of the stream, you are surrounded and unified with billions of other drops. You are pushed on with all the stupendous power of all the other drops which form the stream —*for each drop of water in a Niagara is backed up by ALL the power of ALL the water of that stupendous and gigantic stream.*

If a drop is separated from the stream, it has no power; but, in the stream—unified in action with the stream—it has all power.

You and God flow outward forever, together. You are in His stream of power. You cannot get out of His stream of power. You are in the midst of it—in a stream as great as a million Niagaras flowing out from God, powerfully and irresistibly unified in action in one great outward flow! You cannot get out of that stream. It completely surrounds you and empowers you with all of its power. Being part of the infinite flow, you are backed up by all power at all times—backed up by all the power of God Himself.

When you feel any lack of power, don't try to bolster yourself by using "big" statements of Truth, but instead think of *unified action* of power. Think of yourself as a drop in a gigantic stream of stupendous power, and then realize that all the power of that stream is pushing you on to do what you need to do. This is the understanding which endows you with real consciousness of power.

"Just as every drop of Niagara is backed by all the power of its waters because it is IN the mighty stream, so I am backed by all the power of God, because I am in His stream of power—flowing out from Him forever—and nothing can stop His power."

"All power is given unto me in heaven and in earth." (83)

PART IV

To Gather The Fruit

WON'T YOU SUP WITH ME?

YOU HAVE walked into my dining room, glimpsed some of the beauty there, and taken enough notice of the food on the table to recognize a viand here, a fruit there, and a delicious drink or two—in other words, you have *read* this little book.

And now, I ask you to join me at the table, to partake of the food—in fact, to be my guest for a month, a year, or as long as you wish—to sup with me—so that we shall be sustained day by day.

Reading this book is merely *glancing* at the food.

Studying it and using it is breaking the bread of Truth and sipping the sacred wine of the Spirit.

I do urge you to sup with me—to *use* this little book, and to use it daily.

Christ went often by Himself to pray—to re-affirm His unity with God, and just as He needed spiritual sustenance, so you need it—daily and sometimes hourly. Help of this kind includes affirmations, demands, denials, et cetera. They sustain and strengthen you from hour to hour. The best of these, I give in Lessons 1 to 10, inclusive.

And just as a captain's effort to guide his ship is more confused by fog than by anything else, so in life nothing makes your effort seem so hopelessly confused as a fog of vague ideas. But what joy when sunlight breaks through to your mind and heart, for "Understanding is a wellspring of life." (84) Helps of this kind, I give in Lessons 11 to 19 inclusive.

And since the soul is infinite, it longs to *grow* in expression. So other helps are needed. These I give in Lessons 20 to 31. They are to be used when you have time to meditate and commune with God—to consummate that mystic marriage of spirit and action which gives birth to actuality.

There are *thirty one* methods in this book, so that there is a different one for every day of each month—for every day of even the longest month of the year.

Lesson 1 is to be studied and used on the *first* day of each month; Lesson

2 is to be used on the second day of each month; Lesson 7 on the *seventh* day, et cetera.

And the Lessons are to be used *each* month of the year, and for as many years as you need them—for life!

Moreover, do not limit yourself or limit the use of any particular lesson to any particular day.

If, at any time—during any week, or any day, or any hour—you need the help of any particular lesson, turn to that lesson, and study it at that particular time.

I also urge you to use, each day, one of the Divine "Prescriptions" which follow. They are the only ones, so far as I know, which are made up completely of passages from God's Word.

THIRTY-ONE DIVINE "PRESCRIPTIONS"

(Compounded of God's Word and Christ's Love)

For ABUNDANCE: "The Lord is my Shepherd; I shall not want;" (85) "It is he that giveth———power to get wealth;" (86) "All things that the Father hath are mine." (87)

For BEAUTY: "Arise, shine; for

thy light is come;" (88) "And let the beauty of the Lord our God be upon us;" (89) "For then shalt thou light up thy face without spot." (90)

For CALMNESS: "Be still and know that I am God;" (91) "The eternal God is thy refuge, and underneath are the everlasting arms." (92)

For COURAGE: "I will not be afraid of ten thousands of people, that have set themselves against me round about;" (93) "In God have I put my trust; I will not be afraid what man can do unto me." (94)

For FAITH: "All things, whatsoever ye shall ask in prayer, believing, ye shall receive;" (95) "For with God all things are possible." (96)

For FREEDOM: "Ye have been called into liberty;" (97) "The truth shall make you free;" (98) "Therefore if any man be in Christ, he is a new creature; old things have passed away, all things have become new." (99)

For FRIENDS: "A friend loveth at all times;" (100) "A man that hath friends must show himself friendly;" (101) "Let us love one another; for love is of God." (102)

For GROWTH: "Thou shalt love the Lord thy God with all thine heart;" (103) "Thou shalt love thy neighbor as thyself." (104)

For GUIDANCE: "The Lord is nigh unto all———that call upon him in truth;" (105) "I will go before thee, and make the crooked places straight." (106)

For HARMONY IN BUSINESS: "The Lord shall fight for you, and ye shall hold your peace;" (107) "Love is the fulfilling of the law." (108)

For HARMONY IN THE HOME: "Let all your things be done with charity;" (109) "And my people shall dwell in a peaceable habitation;" (110) "Joy and gladness shall be found therein, thanksgiving, and the voice of melody." (111)

For HEALING: "I will pour out my spirit upon all flesh;" (112) "Behold I will bring it health and a cure;" (113) "I will take sickness away from the midst of thee." (114)

For HEARING: "Say unto them—the ears of the deaf shall be unstopped;" (115) "Then he openeth the ears of men." (116)

For JOY: "Rejoice and be exceeding glad;" (117) "Let them ever shout for joy;" (118) "O let the nations be glad and sing for joy." (119)

For LIFE: "The Spirit of God hath made me, and the breath of the Almighty hath given me life;" (120) "I will give unto him that is athirst of the fountain of the water of life freely." (121)

For LOVE: "See that ye love one another with a pure heart fervently;" (122) "And love, be multiplied." (123)

For MATESHIP: "I will betroth thee unto me forever." (124)

For PASSING ON: "I am the resurrection and the life;" (125) "I give unto them eternal life; and they shall never perish." (126)

For PEACE WITHIN SELF: "I will both lay me down in peace, and sleep; for thou, Lord, only makest me dwell in safety;" (127) "Peace, be still." (128)

For PEACE WITH OTHERS: "We know that to them that love God, all things work together for good;" (129) "The wolf shall dwell with the lamb;" (130) "When a man's ways please the

Lord, he maketh even his enemies to be at peace with him." (131)

For PERFECTION: "Wisdom that is from above is first pure, then peaceable, gentle, and easy to be intreated, full of mercy and good fruits, without partiality, and without hypocrisy;" (132) "Now are we the sons of God, and it doth not yet appear what we shall be." (133)

For POSITION: "Love not sleep, lest thou come to poverty; open thine eyes, and thou shalt be satisfied with bread;" (134) "He shall deliver the needy when he crieth." (135)

For POWER: "God hath not given us the spirit of fear; but of power;" (136) "I can do all things through Christ which strengthen me;" (137) "All power is given unto me in heaven and in earth." (138)

For PROTECTION: "He that dwelleth in the secret place of the Most High shall abide under the shadow of the Almighty;" (139) "My God hath sent his angel, and hath shut the lions' mouths;" (140) "There shall no evil befall thee." (141)

For REST: "And God said, My presence shall go with thee, and I will give thee rest;" (142) "This is my rest forever." (143)

For SIGHT: "The eyes of the blind shall see out of obscurity;" (144) "The eyes of the blind shall be opened," (145) "Receive thy sight; thy faith hath saved thee." (146)

For STRENGTH: "The Lord is the strength of my life;" (147) "He maketh my way perfect." (148)

For UNDERSTANDING: "If any of you lack wisdom, let him ask of God that giveth to all men liberally;" (149) and "Search the scriptures; for in them ye think ye have eternal life." (150)

For UNITY WITH GOD: "I and my Father are one;" (151) "For he dwelleth with you and shall be in you." (152)

For YOU: "I know whence I came and whither I go;" (153) "Behold, the kingdom of God is within you." (154)

For YOUTHFULNESS: "Marvel not that I said unto thee, Ye must be born again;" (155) "His flesh came again like unto the flesh of a little child;" (156) "I will heal thee——— and I will add unto thy days"; (157) "Mine age is departed, and is removed from me as a shepherd's tent;" (158)

PART V

Appendix

LIST OF SOURCES

Each number in parenthesis, found after a line or paragraph in quotation marks, indicates the source from which the quotation is taken. To each such source, I render grateful appreciation:

1—Arnold (Edwin)
2—Wilcox
3—Wilcox
4—Whitman
5—Matthew 17:20
6—Arnold (Matthew)
7—Landone
8—Whitman
9—Luke 4:18
10—Browning (Eliz.)
11—Kneeland
12—Gilman
13—Proverbs 16:3
14—Isaiah 43:1
15—I Corinthians 3:8
16—Fitz Simmons
17—Wilcox
18—Romans 13:10
19—Markham
20—Burroughs
21—Wilcox
22—Romans 12:2
23—Job 22:28
24—Wilcox
25—Browning (Robert)
26—Genesis 1:26
27—I John 3:1
28—Wilcox
29—Isaiah 65:24
30—Matthew 6:32
31—Emerson
32—Proverbs 4:7
33—John 1:3
34—Whitman
35—Genesis 1:31
36—Isaiah 65:18
37—Gilman
38—Zephaniah 3:17
39—Markham
40—John 17:2
41—Arnold (Edwin)
42—Whitman
43—Markham
44—Matthew 5:8
45—Browning (Robert)
46—Pope
47—Matthew 7:1
48—Browning (Robt.)
49—Anon
50—Psalms 91:1
51—Anon
52—Proverbs 10:29
53—Rowell
54—Jeremiah 31:13
55—Carpenter
56—Hay
57—James 2:14
58—Psalms 31:24
59—Realf
60—Tagore
61—Isaiah 41:10
62—Whitman
63—Luke 6:40
64—Longfellow
65—Romans 8:14
66—Van Dyke
67—Luke 17:21
68—Henley
69—Psalms 105:21
70—Gilman

71—Goethe
72—Romans 2:6
73—Exodus 33:14
74—Psalms 72:8
75—Loveman
76—Psalms 27:6
77—Wilcox
78—I Corinthians 16:13
79—Burroughs
80—Matthew 21:22
81—John 14:17
82—Carpenter
83—Matthew 28:18
84—Proverbs 16:22
85—Psalms 23:1
86—Deuteronomy 8:18
87—John 16:15
88—Isaiah 60:1
89—Psalms 90:17
90—Job 11:15
91—Psalms 46:10
92—Deuteronomy 33:27
93—Psalms 3:6
94—Psalms 56:11
95—Matthew 21:22
96—Mark 10:27
97—Galatians 5:13
98—John 8:32
99—II Corinthians 5:17
100—Proverbs 17:17
101—Proverbs 18:24
102—I John 4:7
103—Deuteronomy 6:5
104—Leviticus 19:18
105—Psalms 145:18
106—Isaiah 45:2
107—Exodus 14:14
108—Romans 13:10
109—I Corinthians 16:14
110—Isaiah 32:18
111—Isaiah 51:3
112—Joel 2:28
113—Jeremiah 33:6
114—Exodus 23:25
115—Isaiah 35:5
116—Job 33:16
117—Matthew 5:12
118—Psalms 5:11
119—Psalms 67:4
120—Job 33:4
121—Revelation 21:6
122—I Peter 1:22
123—Jude 2
124—Hosea 2:19
125—John 11:25
126—John 10:28
127—Psalms 4:8
128—Mark 4:39
129—Romans 8:28
130—Isaiah 11:6
131—Proverbs 16:7
132—James 3:17
133—I John 3:2
134—Proverbs 20:13
135—Psalms 72:12
136—II Timothy 1:7
137—Philippians 4:13
138—Matthew 28:18
139—Psalms 91:1
140—Daniel 6:22
141—Psalms 91:10
142—Exodus 33:14
143—Psalms 132:14
144—Isaiah—29:18
145—Isaiah 35:5
146—Luke 18:42
147—Psalms 27:1
148—II Samuel 22:33
149—James 1:5
150—John 5:39
151—John 10:30
152—John 14:17
153—John 8:14
154—Luke 17:21
155—John 3:7
156—II Kings 5:14
157—II Kings 20:5,6
158—Isaiah 38:12

CPSIA information can be obtained
at www.ICGtesting.com
Printed in the USA
LVHW101031251021
701032LV00028B/77

9 781169 239869